first
names

Emmeline
PANKHURST

WHO WILL YOU GET TO KNOW NEXT?

COMING SOON ...

PANKHURST

Haydn Kaye

Illustrations by Michael Cotton-Russell

First Names: EMMELINE PANKHURST
is a
DAVID FICKLING BOOK

First published in Great Britain in 2018 by
David Fickling Books,
31 Beaumont Street,
Oxford, OX1 2NP

Text © Haydn Kaye, 2018
Illustrations © Michael Cotton-Russell, 2018
Cover illustration © Mike Smith, 2018

978-1-910989-61-6

1 3 5 7 9 10 8 6 4 2

Papers used by David Fickling Books are from well-managed
forests and other responsible sources.

Mixed Sources
Product group from well-managed
forests and other controlled sources
www.fsc.org Cert no. TT-COC-2139
FSC © 1996 Forest Stewardship Council

DAVID FICKLING BOOKS Reg. No. 8340307

A CIP catalogue record for this book is available from the British Library.

Printed and bound in Great Britain by Clays Ltd, St Ives plc.

Some of the speech bubbles in this book contain actual
quotes from Emmeline and other important people. You'll
be able to tell which ones they are by the style of type:
'I'd rather be a rebel than a slave.'

CONTENTS

Introduction – Emmeline Hears Something Strange

THE PLACE: A big family house just outside the city of Manchester, England.
THE TIME: Around the year 1870.

Emmeline couldn't get to sleep. She didn't know why, she just couldn't. Hours seemed to pass and still she lay awake. Finally she heard the stairs creak. Now it had to be *really* late – her mum and dad were coming to bed.

But Emmeline's parents didn't go straight to their room. Instead they went to check on all their other children and cooed sweet nothings over each little snoring bundle in turn. Emmeline had nine brothers and sisters, so this seemed to go on for hours.

Emmeline began to wonder: What would they say about *me* if I was asleep? Something glowing, surely. I'm such a helpful girl, and people are always saying how good I am at things. At last she heard her parents tiptoeing up to her bedside.

Suddenly she had an idea. She shut her eyes tight, breathed slowly and steadily, and pretended to be out for the count. Then she lay still and waited for the heaps of praise to come her way. **And she waited. And waited...**

Something was wrong. Why were her parents just standing there saying nothing? Emmeline's heart thumped. Had she done something to upset them? What was it? Her dad sighed and turned to go. And only then, as he stepped out of the room, did he say in the softest, saddest voice to Emmeline's mum:

What a pity she wasn't born a lad.

What on earth do you mean? Emmeline wanted to shout after him. Are boys supposed to be better than girls or something!

But she didn't shout. She couldn't. She was too puzzled by what she'd heard, and quite upset by it too. But in the days that followed she started noticing that her dad wasn't the only one who said such things. Just about everybody seemed to think men mattered more than women – and lots of wives didn't seem to mind acting like their husbands' servants either.

That felt horribly unfair to Emmeline. So when she grew up she decided to speak out about it, on behalf of women everywhere . . .

FLYING THE FLAG FOR ALL FEMALES

'Women are as good as men!' Emmeline protested loud and clear. 'Women should be men's equals, not their slaves!' And she got thrown into prison for saying it, again and again. So, in protest, **she very nearly starved herself to death**!

Newspapers all over the world reported her every move. Not just what she did herself, but what she inspired an army of her female fans to do – because in spite of hating all violence, Emmeline started a kind of war. It was a war to get women treated as men's equals so that life could be better for everyone. In a heartfelt speech at London's Albert Hall in 1912 she declared that her army was on a mission:

9

Although she was very small (her shoe size was just three and a half), Emmeline liked to think big. In her fight for a fair deal for women she gave everything she'd got, and never once stopped believing she would win . . .

Now just hold your horses! I don't much like the start of this story.

I'm sorry?

You made it sound as if my father didn't like me!

Oh, I didn't mean . . .

He adored me! And what he said that night was really his way of paying me a compliment — however odd it might sound today.

I was about to explain that in the next chapter . . .

And I didn't just protest all the time, either. You won't forget to mention that I also had the most wonderful husband, and no fewer than nine children?

It's all going to be in here. Your family, your fame, your long fight for freedom . . .

Oh, is it?

The whole roller-coaster life of The Amazing Emmeline – from girl to granny, from English housewife to worldwide megastar!

Well then, what are we waiting for? On with my story. Chop chop!

1   EMMELINE FALLS OUT WITH HER FATHER

Parents aren't supposed to have favourites, but everyone knew little Emmeline Goulden was her dad's. She was never any trouble, and she was good at all sorts of stuff – like being able to read before she was four years old. When she was a bit older, she would **read the morning paper to her dad** while he ate his breakfast.

There were five girls in the Goulden family. Emmeline, born in 1858, was the eldest. Growing up, she spent lots of time helping her mum to look after the other girls and her five younger brothers too. She really was the family's top child, **the Golden Goulden**.

My brothers would call me The Dictionary because I seemed to know everything!

What does antidisestablishmentarianism mean, Emmeline?

The family lived in a detached white house called Seedley Cottage. It wasn't really a cottage – it was actually much bigger and more comfortable than most other people's houses at that time. There were plenty of fields and woods nearby for the kids to have fun in, as well as the cottage's own rolling gardens, but the busy city of Manchester wasn't far away.

The world back then was massively different from now. There were no cars or bikes, so if any of the Gouldens wanted to travel quickly to Manchester or further away, they had to use a horse. Think of all the things you have to plug into electric sockets today. Not a single one of them had been invented in Emmeline's time.

There were no cinemas either, but there were theatres, where the Goulden children loved to watch their dad get up on stage and act in plays. Acting was just a hobby for him; his day job was running a clothes factory. He'd started out as an errand boy and worked his way up to become the boss, but he never forgot how hard life had been for him at the beginning, and like Emmeline's mum he did whatever he could to help other people who were still struggling.

Emmeline was proud of her dad's achievements, and he was proud of hers. On top of that, **they loved each other to bits**.

But however much they really love each other, dads and daughters don't always see eye to eye over everything . . .

THE TRUTH DAWNS ON EMMELINE

Even a girl as clever as Emmeline had to go to school. She was, of course, near the top of her class. But she'd always noticed something odd about what happened at school, and after a while it began to annoy her. The boys had lessons like we have today, but she and the other girls were forever being given tips on how to be 'ladylike' – how to make the home nice for their male relations by dusting furniture, arranging flowers, and that kind of thing.

This puzzled Emmeline because no one taught her brothers how to make the house look nice for their sisters. It didn't seem fair.

Something else puzzled and irritated her too. There was no end of talk about all her brothers' job prospects. One was going to help their dad to run the factory, another would be a painter, another an actor . . . **No one ever spoke about what the Goulden girls might do when they grew up**. For a while Emmeline really couldn't work out what was going on. Then at last she got it:

Oh, right! People really do think boys are better than girls!

14

When girls became women in the 1800s, they had nothing like the same chances in life as men – even though they were perfectly capable of doing the things men did. That's why Emmeline's dad had whispered those strange words that night in her bedroom.

What he actually meant was that Emmeline was so talented, she'd have been brilliant at any career. But in Britain 150 years ago, **only men got to do really interesting jobs**. Women were just starting to be trained up for nursing careers, there was no secretarial work for them, shop assistants were all men, and no woman could be a doctor, a lawyer or an architect – Emmeline couldn't even go to university and get a degree. Some women did write for a living, but to be taken seriously, a few of them pretended to be male authors!

Emmeline didn't much like the idea of that, and it sounded even worse when she found out what most women were expected to do with their lives instead.

How To Be A Household Machine

Girls from families like Emmeline's were supposed to do three main things after leaving school:

1. Find a husband. 2. Have some babies. 3. Stay at home and make the house look nice.

As it happened, plenty of women were quite happy with that – though they really didn't have much choice. Even so, being married 150 years ago wasn't like being married today. Men could rule over their wives like mini kings. Not long before Emmeline's time, it was said that a judge – who was a man, naturally – decreed that it was fine for a husband to beat his wife, but that the stick should be **no thicker than his thumb**!

Housework too was nothing like it is today. Machines like dishwashers and microwaves and vacuum cleaners and washing machines didn't exist. Imagine having to wash every last item of your family's clothing, by hand, at a sink!

The only real machine in the house was the woman herself.

My dear, the baby's crying.

Emmeline's mum, Mrs Goulden, was lucky. She could afford to pay people to help her do all the exhausting chores, but she explained to her children how tough it was for most women to look after their kids and run a home. Wives from families far poorer than the Gouldens had to do all this work with hardly any money, in horribly cramped little homes, **with no help whatever** from either humans or machines.

Just the thought of all that upset Emmeline. But she didn't protest. Not yet. Back then, she just thought this was the way things were, and these were 'the rules' that girls and women had always followed. She didn't yet realize that sometimes rules could change.

But already it seemed staggeringly unfair to her that only men got to do exciting and worthwhile jobs.

However, she still had a few years left to enjoy herself.

Emmeline Falls In Love With France

Emmeline's dad often went abroad on business. When Emmeline was 14 – and still the apple of his eye – he took her with him to France on one of his trips.

She absolutely loved it all. French sights, French smells, French people, French fashions – especially the fashions. She spent hours just gazing into shop windows. She loved it all so much that as soon as she got home **she begged to go back again**.

Her dad could see how keen she was, so he arranged for Emmeline to go to a finishing school in Paris. In those days lots of rich parents did this with their daughters. Basically it meant the girls 'finished' their education abroad. Then they would be ready to come home, get married and settle down.

I was only 14 years old. Marriage still seemed ages away and Paris was so exciting!

18

Almost as soon as she got to Paris, Emmeline made a new best friend, a French girl called Noemie. Her father was a nobleman who'd been banished overseas for fighting for the rights of ordinary people. That gave the girls something in common, since they'd both been brought up to believe that posh families like theirs shouldn't just enjoy their good luck in life – they should help the less fortunate too.

Emmeline and Noemie did everything together – exploring the city's cafés and museums, discussing art and books, window shopping till their eyes ached.

A woman's place is definitely in Paris.

Emmeline didn't bother too much with lessons, though these were much less 'girly' than her lessons back in England, with classes on things like chemistry and keeping accounts. She just didn't rate any schools, and she never really believed they were the best places for children to learn.

By talking so much with Noemie, Emmeline could soon speak French pretty well. The girls never doubted they would be friends for life, so they made all sorts of plans for the future. They agreed that if they ever had daughters, they would swap them over now and then when they were teenagers. Then each could learn the other's language and find out far more about the other's country than they would in any dreary old school.

ALL GOOD THINGS COME TO AN END (DON'T THEY?)

For five fabulous years Emmeline went back and forth to France. By the age of 19, with her black hair, olive-coloured skin and deep violet-blue eyes, she cut a wonderfully stylish figure in her smart Parisian clothes. And though she was small, she stood up so straight that she made herself seem much taller. Even her voice was a thing of beauty. When she spoke, people said it **sounded like she was singing**!

Now, though, her schooling was over. She was 'finished'. There was nothing for her to do except return to Britain. And once she was home, there wasn't much else for her to do except help out around the house, especially with all the smaller children. That was what tended to happen to young women from Emmeline's kind of family before they got themselves hitched up to a husband.

So back again at Seedley Cottage, she became a kind of trainee household machine. Life was so dull. She missed France terribly; she missed Noemie. Manchester could be an exciting place – but oh, **how could she live without Paris**?

She racked her brains for a way to get back there, and after a year or so she hit on a plan. One of Emmeline's younger sisters, Mary, was about to be sent to France for finishing. Emmeline pleaded with her dad to let her go too – you know, just to keep an eye on little Mary, make sure she didn't get into trouble. **Her dad said yes**!

EMMELINE HATCHES ANOTHER PLAN

At once Emmeline got back together with Noemie. Off they went again around the shops and cafés and galleries of Paris. They chattered away together non-stop – about politics as well as about culture, just as they'd done with their parents while they were growing up. But posh young women in France were expected to get married, just as they were in England – so that's what Noemie had done. Her new husband was a painter from Switzerland, and already they'd had a baby daughter.

Now Emmeline had a long hard think about all this.

Noemie did seem a bit young to be a wife. But she also seemed happy, and her little baby girl was **utterly lovely**. Emmeline didn't particularly want to get married, but there didn't seem any way out of it. So if she had to follow those 'rules' and become somebody's wife, she decided she might as well find a husband who would help her to stay in France. Then she could stay close to Noemie, and their families could grow up together. It seemed like making the best of a bad job. There would also be all the fun of wearing a beautifully fashionable dress on her wedding day.

Emmeline always liked getting on with things, so she shared her idea at once with Noemie, who thought it made **perfect sense**. It mightn't sound a very romantic plan to us today, but Emmeline had become so bored waiting hand and foot on her brothers in England. Admittedly, as a wife she would have to wait on her husband, but at least she would then be running her own home – and she planned to open up that home to as many interesting and important people as possible, people who might go on to help change the world for the better.

Noemie introduced Emmeline to a French writer and in no time he agreed to make the clever English girl with the sweet smile his bride. But it wasn't just Emmeline's looks or brains that won him over – he had also heard she came from quite a rich family, so before he agreed to 'tie the knot', he had a request. Would she please bring him **a nice fat bag of money from her father**?

Emmeline was sure this would be fine with her dad. She was, after all, the Golden Goulden. And lots of dads in the 1800s paid a 'dowry' when their daughters got married. This was, basically, a kind of bribe. A father paid it to a future groom's family so his daughter could be 'taken off his hands' – in other words, so he wouldn't have to carry on paying for her upkeep. Some brides were then allowed to dip into the cash themselves, which meant they didn't have to keep asking hubby every time they wanted an ice cream or a new hat. (And Emmeline had always hated seeing her mum hand every household bill to her dad to pay.)

Expecting no difficulties, she wrote home to her dad asking for the dosh.

Back To Earth With A Bump

Emmeline's father went ballistic.

He didn't just refuse to sell his 'own daughter for money', as he put it. He also said he didn't want her marrying any old foreigner – and he definitely didn't want her living abroad. In fact, since the rest of the family was away on holiday and the housekeeper was off sick, he ordered Emmeline back from Paris **straight away** to look after him and Seedley Cottage.

Throughout her life, Emmeline never liked taking no for an answer. But back to Manchester she had to go – with her plans all in tatters, and hopping mad at her dad. As she went back through the cottage door, she was quite possibly the angriest trainee household machine in Britain! But she didn't have to stay furious for long.

The year was 1879, Emmeline was 21, and her life was about to change **for ever**.

2   Emmeline Finds True Love

Emmeline was standing in a crowd on a Manchester street when a horse-drawn cab drew to a halt. She glimpsed the hand of the male passenger inside as he reached out to open the door. It was just a hand – but Emmeline was struck by what a very beautiful hand it was. She **held her breath** to see who would emerge . . .

Call The Doctor

The man who climbed out was almost as old as Emmeline's dad. He wasn't very tall and he looked a bit untidy, a pointy red beard covering half of his face. Above the beard, his eyes were small and beady, and when he spoke to the cab driver, his voice was surprisingly squeaky. In short, his hand was quite easily his best feature.

That didn't matter to Emmeline. Nor did it matter to the crowd who were already clapping and cheering. Because this was Richard Marsden Pankhurst, known to everyone as The Doctor (a doctor of law, not medicine) and he'd come to give a talk. The Doctor was well known in Manchester for speaking up for the poor, the sick, the jobless and the old – all people who got precious little help with their daily struggles back in the 1800s.

When Richard made his speech, his squeaky voice swept Emmeline away. So did the **passion and fire** she heard in every word he said.

She'd just liked the look of his hand to begin with, but she went home to her parents' house liking everything about him. Yes, it was true he was more than twice her age. But he was such a fine man, and he had such noble plans to make life fairer. That money-grabbing French writer hadn't touched Emmeline's heart at all. The Doctor was entirely different. So she wrote to him to get his views on women's education, but secretly also to find out if he was **just as wonderful** in private as he appeared to be in public.

EMMELINE GETS HER MAN

Soon letters were flying back and forth between them. And when they actually met, Emmeline was bowled over by Richard and Richard was bowled over by Emmeline. She loved how he treated her like a true equal (why weren't all men so sensible?). Luckily for Emmeline too, her dad didn't have a problem with Richard: he'd already met The Doctor and thoroughly approved of the way he stood up for the weak and poor.

But Emmeline's mum wasn't so sure. Richard still lived with his parents and he didn't have many of the more practical skills most men were expected to have . . .

Ggnnnhh

He didn't even mind that he wasn't the kind of man women queued up to marry. 'I am a helpless creature!' he'd happily say.

Nothing could stand in the way of **true love**, though, and in no time Emmeline and Richard got engaged. Then Richard's parents both died very suddenly, and though they were old, their deaths were still a huge shock to him. Emmeline felt he needed something joyful in his life, and quickly set a date for the wedding.

But Richard was so grief-stricken that it didn't seem right to have a big, noisy, fun-packed day. Only a few guests were invited to the small church ceremony.

Emmeline didn't even wear a white dress – to match Richard's mood, she wore a brown one instead. It wasn't very flattering, but on 18th December 1879 Emmeline didn't give two hoots for high fashion. She'd just become the proud new Mrs Pankhurst, and the man she loved **with all her soul** was surely heading for the top.

She vowed to do all she could to help him succeed, because in the 1800s that's what a wife was expected to do: stand by her man and make him greater. And years later the name Pankhurst *would* go down in history. But it wouldn't be Richard who made it famous . . .

No Household Machines Here!

The Doctor and The Dictionary made a perfect pair. As husband and wife, they were blissfully happy. Richard was so unlike most other men: he saw his wife as his equal in every way, and wanted her with him as he went around speaking up for the less fortunate. No way did he want Emmeline to be a household machine. Together they were **Team Pankhurst**.

Emmeline's dad felt Richard should have been putting in more time at his day job – as a lawyer – to give him a chance of one day becoming a well-paid judge. But right then the newly-weds were so hard up, Emmeline asked her dad for a second time if she could have a dowry.

Mr Goulden's views on this rather touchy subject hadn't changed, and for a second time he said no. Emmeline was so mad, she hardly ever spoke to him again. She didn't care. She was no longer interested in being a Golden Goulden – now she wanted to be a **Perfect Pankhurst**.

The Patter Of (Lots Of) Tiny Feet

Emmeline moved south with Richard, to London, where he planned to crank up his campaigning for the poor. Right away she set up a small shop to bring in some extra cash, calling it Emerson's, and selling fancy goods like teapots and picture frames. Meanwhile Team Pankhurst was growing in size fast. Richard and Emmeline hadn't been married a year before baby number one arrived. She was the **sweetest little girl** and they called her Christabel.

Within two years Christabel had a sister, Sylvia, for company, and two years after that, their brother Frank arrived. Yet another baby girl, Adela, was born the next year.

TEAM PANKHURST

Christabel   Sylvia   Frank   Adela

Emmeline had now given birth four times in under five years. All those kids, as well as running the shop, kept her on her toes, though once again she was luckier than many new mums – she could afford to hire a nursemaid called Susannah to help with the children, and later she sometimes paid governesses to give them lessons. Emmeline was grateful too when her sister

Mary – who hadn't yet got married – offered to lend a hand and soon became what the kids called their 'deputy mother'.

Emmeline loved every minute of her new family life. She especially loved being Christabel's mum. Like her own dad, Emmeline couldn't help having a favourite, and right from the start, Christabel was her **number one child** in every way.

But in September 1888 disaster struck her only son. One afternoon in London, the children were taken out for a walk. Or rather, the three older ones walked while poor little three-year-old Adela had to be pushed in a pram. She'd been born with weak legs, and when she did learn to walk, she had to wear iron splints. Her brother Frank had seemed fine, prancing along beside the pram pretending to be a horse.

But when they got home, Frank went down with a sudden nasty cough. Two different doctors tried to help, but they didn't realize how sick the boy was. He had diphtheria, a serious disease that children are vaccinated against today. Children in Frank's time were not so lucky.

Later that week, frightening moans woke up the Pankhurst girls in the middle of the night. The sound was coming from Frank's bedroom, but it wasn't Frank making it – it was Emmeline. She'd just found her dear young son **dead in his bed**.

Frank Comes Back!

It's torture for any parent to lose a young child. This was the first big loss of Emmeline's life, and it broke her heart. She could fight her feelings only by pretending Frank had never existed. She shut away her pictures of him in a bedroom cupboard and wouldn't let anyone so much as say his name.

That may sound a bit harsh of her, but Emmeline never saw any point in moping about. Above all else, **the show had to go on** – and she aimed to keep Team Pankhurst marching at the double into a brilliantly successful future.

The very next year, the Team did get something new to celebrate. Emmeline's doctor told her she was going to have another baby. Now, at last, Emmeline did mention her dead son's name. And when she gave birth to a healthy baby boy, she even called him Francis Henry, which had also been Frank's names. That was a bit too much for Richard and the

It's Frank. He's coming again!

Er . . . are you feeling all right, my dear?

rest of the family to bear, so everyone called him Harry instead.

Now the team was complete. Two loving parents: Richard and Emmeline; and four delightful children: Christabel, Sylvia, Adela and Harry. But there could only ever be one team captain – **and that wasn't Richard** . . .

EMMELINE CALLS THE SHOTS

Richard kept moving the family from place to place for his work. But he still didn't do much around the house. He couldn't even carve the joint of meat on a Sunday – the only day of the week when the whole family ate together. And when he did talk to the kids, it could sound like one of his speeches.

If you do not grow up to help other people, you will not have been worth bringing up!

Most of the time, he was happy to let Emmeline rule the roost. And her rule was fairly strict. So even though Sylvia and Harry had poor eyesight, she wouldn't let either of them wear glasses. Strangely, she just **didn't believe glasses worked**. This gave both children quite a few problems as they got older.

Emmeline didn't believe in religion either. So unlike most other British parents at that time, she didn't bring her kids up as Christians. A third thing she didn't believe in, after her own underwhelming education, was sending children to primary school. High school might just about work for them, but primary? No way.

You can stay at home and teach each other!

Emmeline didn't want her kids to be taught just the same old boring facts as other children. And there was no need whatever for them to learn 'ladylike' behaviour. She talked and read to them about things that interested her, and got them to meet friends of hers and Richard's who also had interesting things to say. The rest of the time, she spoke to her daughters and son like mini adults. She expected them to behave like mini adults too. They even had to go to their parents' parties. In some ways, Emmeline really couldn't wait for them all to grow up.

The kids did love their mum and dad. But it wasn't that much fun being at home the whole day through, and they were often squabbling. So it was quite a relief for them to go to high school at last, and make some friends outside Team Pankhurst . . .

I know I asked you to mention my children, but that is enough of them now. At that time their father, my dear Richard, was much more important.

Yes, I was about to—

Please don't interrupt. You need to say how he went into politics. So that he could help even more people.

But first I need to explain to the readers how politics worked in your time.
The suffrage, Parliament, and so on.
It really was quite complicated . . .

Then leave the explaining to me. It's really not complicated at all . . .

EMMELINE EXPLAINS POLITICS

Shh, Your Majesty, we are trying to run the country.

I'm here too!

Politics is all about the way countries are run. Britain in the 1800s wasn't ruled by kings and queens, the way it had been in olden times. There was still a queen – Victoria – but now she was mainly just for show.

The person who was really in charge was the Prime Minister, just like today, and the politicians who helped him to run the country were his 'Government', and had to be elected. Here's how:

Are you calling me an ornament!

A vote for me means a cheaper loaf of bread!

Conservative Candidate

Vote for me and I'll make the trains run faster!

Liberal Candidate

Ballot Box

British politics was based on the 'suffrage'. The term comes from an old Latin word meaning the right anyone has to vote. At election time, a voter put his vote in the box to say which politician he was choosing from his local area to help to run the country. Most of these politicians belonged to two main parties: the Conservatives and the Liberals. Each party was made up of men who had similar views. All the votes in the area were counted up and the winning politician went off to Westminster, in London, to be a Member of Parliament – or MP for short.

This happened all over the country. As a result, around 650 new MPs gathered together in the House of Commons, where the laws of the land (called Acts of Parliament) were made.

It was all much simpler when royals ruled.

And much more unfair.

Meanwhile, the party with the most MPs was declared the overall winner, and its leader became the Prime Minister. He then formed a Government — the group of MPs that helped him with the day-to-day running of the country — which takes us neatly back to the start of this explanation . . .

You haven't mentioned us! I'm the queen's second cousin, don't you know!

I say old boy, do calm down!

Oh very well. There was also a second house of Parliament — the House of Lords. This house had once been important, but like the royal family, it no longer mattered much. No one was elected to it: you were a member only if you already happened to be a 'top' person such as a duke, earl, bishop or archbishop.

Thank you. That was most helpful.

I haven't finished yet. And this last part is absolutely vital . . .

Sorry, Emmeline.

Please note that every single person in my explanation (except for the queen) was a man. **NOT ONE WOMAN**. Just hold that thought for a moment. We will be coming back to it. Now do continue . . .

EMMELINE DECIDES TO GET INVOLVED

To make life better for poorer people, Richard Pankhurst wanted to become an MP. If he got voted into Parliament, he could start making a real difference; by speaking out in the House of Commons, he could convince other politicians that new laws should be made to protect the poor.

That was Richard's plan and Emmeline threw herself into campaigning for him, but though he tried to get elected three times in different parts of the country, **three times he failed** to win enough votes. He never became an MP.

Little Sylvia took her dad's defeats very badly – after the third election she burst into tears when they gave out the result. As soon as they got home Emmeline took her to one side. She said that by showing how upset she was, Sylvia had brought shame on the whole family and if Emmeline hated anything, it was people showing weakness. Team Pankhurst was better than that. Team Pankhurst was **strong, strong, strong**! And no one seemed stronger than Emmeline herself.

After all Richard's defeats, the family moved back to Manchester. He was starting to get weary with life and had serious problems with his stomach, but Emmeline buzzed with energy. One person who met her called her 'lively as a cricket, full of clever comment'. The way Emmeline was starting to see it, to be a wife and mother was a great thing for any woman – it had certainly worked for her – but she still felt she had more to give.

So during her thirties she threw herself into projects outside the home, but not as a shopkeeper this time – she had set her sights a lot higher. In London she'd already helped women and girls who worked in a matchstick factory win safer working conditions from their bosses – help that was desperately needed.

Plenty of others all over the country were crying out for someone to make a difference to their lives too. Emmeline felt furious that although Britain was a wealthy country, so many of its people still lived in poverty – yet hardly anyone seemed to be lifting a finger to improve things.

A MISERABLE LIFE FOR MATCH GIRLS

Only 13 years old

Tired from working long hours in the matchstick factory with hardly any breaks

Phossy Jaw – damaged jaw from breathing in poisonous fumes from the phosphorus used to the make the matches

Small for her age, because she can't afford good food

FINE Dirty Feet

Clothes have bluey-green glow from working with phosphorus

She'd be fined by the factory management for having dirty feet

Richard had done as much as he could to make the world a better place. Maybe now it was time for a woman's voice to be raised against all the unfairness. Emmeline Pankhurst's own years of protest were about to begin . . .

3 EMMELINE FACES SOME HARD FACTS

When Emmeline was growing up, her mum and dad often reminded her how well off the Gouldens were compared to most families. Campaigning with Richard, she found out just how terrible the 'curse of poverty' could be. The Pankhursts were always short of cash, but thousands who lived quite near to them in Manchester were **crushingly poor** – so poor they couldn't survive on their own.

It was the same all across Britain: people who were too old or too sick to work, people who couldn't find a paid job, children whose parents just weren't able to look after them. Today, pensions and welfare payments help to protect vulnerable people, and by law all children are educated until they are 18. That was not the case in the Britain of the 1890s.

Thanks, Mrs P!

Since Emmeline was such a practical woman, she quickly made herself useful. She asked shopkeepers to donate leftover food. This was then made up into soup which she handed out daily to growing crowds of hungry people in Manchester's Stevenson Square.

In 1894 she also got herself elected as a Poor Law Guardian. The work was unpaid, and until that year, you'd had to own property to be allowed to do the job and very few women qualified. As soon as the law changed, in came Emmeline, rolling up her sleeves and ready for action.

But nothing had prepared her for what she would discover over the next four years. The experience shocked her so much that the course of her life changed again . . .

WELCOME TO THE WORKHOUSE

If you didn't have a job and you couldn't pay your bills, you still had to live somewhere. In those days, according to what was called the Poor Law, you'd be sent to stay in a grim workhouse. Just the name struck fear into everyone who heard it. As a Poor Law Guardian, it was one of Emmeline's tasks to help run the workhouse in the Chorlton district of Manchester. **She'd never seen anything so horrific**. The place was like a sprawling great prison: it wasn't just one building, there was also a farm, a 900-bed hospital and lots of workshops. Crowds of men and women were jam-packed inside, some of them so old that all they could do was sit all day – yet all they had to sit on was benches with no backs.

Thin little girls aged seven or eight were down on their knees **scrubbing cold stone floors** for hours on end.

Pregnant women had to scrub too – right up to the moment they gave birth. Two weeks later, they were made to decide whether to go on working their fingers to the bone at the workhouse, separated all day long from their babies, or risk taking their newborns out into the big bad world.

Emmeline couldn't believe these people had nowhere to get a quiet moment. And no one in charge ever had a kind word for them, even though they'd **done nothing wrong**. It was just that poor people often disgusted richer people, and frightened them too. So the richer people's thinking seemed to go like this: if the lives of the less fortunate are made harsher still, they'll want to 'shape up' and become less poor!

Pig Ignorant

Right away Emmeline started sorting a few things out at Chorlton Workhouse.

'I am a very ordinary matter-of-fact person,' she liked to tell people. But she was also **extremely good** at getting things done.

First there was the problem of diet. She found the Guardians mainly gave the inmates great hunks of cheap bread to eat, but the bread was so dry they could never stomach much of it. Emmeline hated seeing food go to waste, so she got the staff to cut the bread into slices and spread it with a new type of food called 'margarine'. This made it easier to eat, and if any bread was then left over, it was mixed with milk and currants to make puddings for the older inmates, who didn't have the teeth for chewing.

Practical, you see? Just a woman's pure common sense.

Emmeline also made sure more vegetables were grown on the workhouse farm for healthy meals. She brought in chairs with backs for the older inmates, and arranged for the girls to have nightdresses, warm winter clothing, and proper underwear. (The matron had been bothered about the girls' clothing for some time, but she'd been too **embarrassed** to say the word 'knickers' to the male Guardians!)

Over four years Emmeline made a huge difference to Chorlton Workhouse, but it was just one workhouse among so many. Emmeline wanted to find a way to change them all, and that meant changing people's ideas about the poor. She'd seen with her own eyes that hardly any of the workhouse inmates were to blame for the trouble they were in. Jobs could be hard to find, and everyone got sick from time to time – so it was just **plain cruel** to treat all these people like criminals.

This was exactly why Richard had so badly wanted to become a Member of Parliament. As an MP he could have helped get rid of the old Poor Law, then drawn up a new law to help the poverty-stricken. If only more voters had had the common sense to vote for him, Emmeline thought. It still baffled her that Richard had lost not just one election but three. What was wrong with those voters?

The answer, she realized, was staring her in the face. The voters were all men!

Astounding as it might seem to us today, ever since British elections had begun back in the mists of time, **NOT ONE WOMAN HAD EVER CAST A VOTE!**

VOTES FOR WOMEN? (IN THEIR DREAMS!)

Before the 1800s, suffrage – like going to university or getting an interesting job – was always seen as purely **men's business**. Women had never voted in the past, so why start now? It seemed to be another one of those old 'rules' of life – and plenty of women as well as men saw no reason to break it.

Why would any woman need to vote?

Her father or brother or husband or even her son is perfectly capable of voting for her!

I completely agree.

Not all British men had the right to vote, though. Until the 1800s, hardly anyone did – you pretty much had to own land or houses to qualify. Then some new laws gave the vote to more men, but still, around the time Richard tried to get elected, four out of every ten men didn't have it. As for women, **ten out of ten** didn't have it. That put them alongside three other vote-less sets of people: kids, male criminals and mentally ill men!

Ever since the 1860s, groups of female 'suffragists' had been politely suggesting (in books, articles and letters to newspapers) that women should have the vote too. The suffragists had support from some men, but not enough from politicians in Parliament. These politicians were the ones who would then be able to change the law to give votes to women. But most of them didn't think a change was needed – at least not yet. Women were told they would have to be patient. They'd always been good at that. Meanwhile the suffragists went on patiently campaigning away.

Oddly enough, one person who wanted **no change ever** for women happened to be a woman herself.

Queen Victoria sat on the British throne for an enormously long time, from 1837 till 1901. She thought the suffragists were mad.

Dear Prime Minister
  Let woman be what God
intended – a helpmate for man,
but with totally different duties.
  Yours faithfully
  Queen Victoria

She could afford to say that. She didn't need a vote to get her voice heard!

EMMELINE MAKES HER POINT

Emmeline got herself really wound up about all this. It was so unfair. Women were **just as capable** as men, and in her opinion they often had a good deal more common sense. They were also likely to be a bit less harsh in their views and opinions than men. Why then shouldn't they be allowed to vote?

It bothered Emmeline as much as the workhouse did. There was just so much wrong with the country that needed putting right; so many old 'rules' that had to change. And she was determined to point all this out – she just had to work out how.

In the 1890s, without TV, the internet or social media, the best way to grab people's attention was to get up and make a speech. So Emmeline decided to put that clear, sing-song voice of hers to good use. At small protest meetings to begin with, she stood up and spoke out about issues affecting the poor. She always felt nervous before she started, but she put her heart and soul into what she said.

Often her teenage daughters came to listen. Christabel and Sylvia saw how worked up their mum got about women's suffrage, and that got them worked up too. No way did they plan to live in a world where women played second fiddle to men – and one day Christabel said something that really stuck in Emmeline's mind: 'How long you women have been trying for the vote! For my part, **I mean to get it**.'

Emmeline wondered if she was right. Maybe women shouldn't just wait patiently for change. Maybe it was time they stopped being quite so polite and started making some noise. Then something happened that made Emmeline really stop and think.

The Heroine Of Boggart Hole Clough

There was an open-air space in Manchester with the strange name of Boggart Hole Clough (pronounced 'Cluff'). On Sundays in the 1890s, thousands of working people met there to hear protest speeches. Emmeline, who was quite well known already as the wife of The Doctor, became one of the regular speakers. The crowds grew so big that the men on Manchester's Parks Committee got jittery . . .

What if all those workers get so worked up that they go on the rampage?

. . . and they banned all meetings at Boggart Hole Clough.

Emmeline wasn't having that.

With other – male – speakers she went on making speeches there, often wearing a pink straw bonnet that marked her out even more among all the men. Massed crowds kept turning up to listen, until the speakers were summoned to court and **ordered to pay a fine** for breaking the law.

Emmeline, along with two of the men, refused to pay up. They all thought the law was ridiculous, but fully expected to be put in jail for not obeying it. Emmeline didn't mind – in fact she said she was happy to spend a night locked away to stick up for her right to speak wherever she liked.

But as it happened, the two men were given short prison sentences and Emmeline wasn't. No one quite knew why. Maybe it was because she was a woman.

Quite a posh woman too. Not at all the kind of person who usually got thrown into jail. Then, to her astonishment, the ban on meetings was quietly dropped!

Interesting. Very interesting . . .

Emmeline had stood up to the men in power and made them back down. By sticking to what she believed in, she'd got her own way – and become **a local heroine**.

Not At All Quiet On The Home Front

Back at home, however, things weren't going quite so well.

Harry had turned into a rather sad little chap. A sickly boy, he longed to spend more time with his parents, but they were always so busy, and his three big sisters were all a bit too old to play with him.

Emmeline's youngest daughter, Adela, was miserable too. At the age of 11 – feeling neglected by her parents – she ran away from home, but luckily didn't get far. Meanwhile her sister Sylvia often looked even more miserable. One of Adela's friends once told her: 'Your face would frighten a crow off its nest!' But Sylvia was really good at drawing and painting. So even while she sulked, she got on with her art. Then there was Christabel, Emmeline's eldest child.

Ah, dear Christabel. Yes, she was a worry to me.

For years she'd dreamed that Christabel – clever at many things, but an especially good dancer – would become a professional ballerina. Then Emmeline herself would proudly accompany her beautiful daughter all around Europe as she performed. But Christabel lost interest in dancing, and aged 18 she just didn't seem to know what to do with her life.

At that point, Emmeline remembered the deal she'd made all those years ago with her old friend Noemie. The time had come for their daughters to start swapping homes.

Noemie now lived with her family in the Swiss city of Geneva. Maybe Christabel would **fall in love** with Europe just like Emmeline had as a young girl. She couldn't fail to enjoy herself anyway. So Emmeline came up with a plan. She would deliver Christabel to Noemie, have a short holiday herself, then head back home.

In June 1898 Emmeline set off from England with her daughter. More than twenty years had passed since she first discovered Paris, so they stopped off there on the way to see the old places Emmeline had loved so long ago. Once they reached Geneva, they settled in well: sunbathing, taking boat trips, going for rides in one of the first-ever motor cars. Emmeline really didn't want to tear herself away. Yet home was where her beloved Richard was.

Hold on to your hats, we're travelling at fifteen miles an hour!

Emmeline had always said her marriage was pretty-well ideal. Over the years, she'd had to face up to many hard facts about life – and through it all Richard Marsden Pankhurst had been her one true shining light.

But as it turned out, **she couldn't have picked a worse time to go abroad** . . .

4   EMMELINE FIGHTS ON ALONE

In Geneva, Emmeline received a telegram from Richard. Before there were texts or emails, telegrams were the quickest way for people to send messages over long distances. Sometimes they brought news worth celebrating. Usually though, they were sent in emergencies, and this message from Richard didn't sound good:

POST OFFICE
TELEGRAM
STAMP
3M

I AM NOT WELL.
PLEASE COME HOME.

Leaving Christabel behind, Emmeline rushed by train for the boat back to England. For years Richard hadn't been in the best of health. He was now 64, quite old for a man in those days, but his digestion was awful and he often had crippling stomach pains. After arriving in London, however, Emmeline got the **shock of her life** when another passenger came into her compartment on the train to Manchester, sat down and opened his newspaper . . .

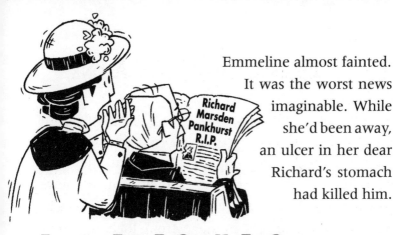

Emmeline almost fainted. It was the worst news imaginable. While she'd been away, an ulcer in her dear Richard's stomach had killed him.

EMMELINE TRIES TO PICK UP THE PIECES

Losing Richard shattered Emmeline.

People who knew her well said she never really got over it. She still had the same sweet smile, but now it was always touched by sadness. At 40 years of age, The Dictionary felt **impossibly lonely** without The Doctor at her side. Lost in sorrow, she thought her world had come to an end.

But although Team Pankhurst had lost its oldest member, the show did have to go on. Emmeline still had four kids to take care of. They too missed their dad terribly – even the smaller ones who'd sometimes been a bit afraid of him. Emmeline also had to make sure enough money was coming in. Richard had been the breadwinner, and he'd left almost no savings, so now she had to get the family finances sorted – fast.

The first thing she did was move the family into a cheaper, pokier little house. And since she wasn't being paid for her job at the workhouse, sadly she had to give it up. Like many women of her time she hadn't been trained for any kind of career, so she tried starting up another shop. Shopkeeping hadn't really made much money for her in London, but maybe it would in Manchester. Hoping for the best, she filled a new branch of Emerson's with silks, cushions and other fancy goods. But at that point, **Emmeline's luck changed**, and along came a more suitable opportunity . . .

LIVING IN A MAN-MADE WORLD

The Chorlton Guardians offered Emmeline a job with a wage, and she grabbed it with both hands. She became a registrar in a very poor district of Manchester, registering all the births and deaths that happened there. (Marriages had to be registered too. But the law said only a male registrar could do this.)

Emmeline still had to devote most of her working time to Emerson's, but she fitted her registry work into a few hours at the start and end of each day. That's when people came to let her know about a birth or a death in their family. Some were terribly poor women, who told Emmeline how glad they were to be dealing with a woman rather than the less friendly men who'd done her job before. They described to her how grim their lives were and their suffering seemed grotesquely unfair.

Emmeline had made such a good job of organizing the schooling of her workhouse children, she was also elected to help run some Manchester schools. Life didn't seem fair here either. Schoolmasters were paid more than schoolmistresses, even though the women did **much more work**. The women didn't just teach sewing and cooking alongside regular lessons, many of them also used their wages to give meals to pupils whose parents couldn't afford to feed them.

One thing was becoming clearer and clearer to Emmeline: women needed a bigger say in how things were done. But in a man-made world, how could they make themselves heard? As the 1800s ended and the 1900s began, old Queen Victoria died and her son became King Edward VII. But for many British people, life just went on being **the same tough old struggle** it had always been.

JOBS FOR THE GIRLS

In Emmeline's personal life, however, things were looking up a bit, because at least she didn't have to worry quite so much about the rest of Team Pankhurst.

Adela enjoyed school so much, she trained to be a teacher – which was seen as a very suitable role for a woman. And Sylvia turned into such a good artist, she was offered a place to study at Manchester's School of Art – though being an artist was not quite so suitable, since most professional artists were still men. But Emmeline proudly put some of Sylvia's paintings up for sale at Emerson's, and Sylvia also made posters for the shop to advertise things like Christmas crackers.

When Emmeline was away, all the girls had to put in shifts serving at Emerson's – including Christabel, back from Noemie's but still at a loose end. Very few customers visited the shop, so to keep her oldest daughter's spirits up Emmeline sent her off to listen to some public lectures. As a result, Christabel made some lively new friends – women who talked non-stop about female suffrage – and in 1903 she decided that what she really wanted was to study law just like her dad. She had no trouble getting into a college, but there was just one hitch: once she had qualified, being a woman, **she wouldn't actually be allowed to work** as a lawyer!

I really do think that's enough about my family. Isn't this MY life story?

But your children played such an important part in it, didn't they?

Hmm. What you really need to talk about now is how I joined the Labour Party. Do you wish me to explain again?

No, I can handle it.
You just sit back and enjoy.

PARTY TIME

In the 1800s the Government was usually formed by politicians from either the Liberal Party or the Conservative Party. For many coal miners, factory labourers or people without jobs, it didn't make much difference. Often they didn't even know which party was ruling. They just knew neither party ever did much to help them.

At last, in around 1900, a party for people like these began to come together. The Labour Party. It seemed so fair-minded and modern – everything Emmeline could have wished for. The Labour Party made all the right noises too about campaigning for a better deal for women. Emmeline was quick to join it. She gave speeches at its meetings, and made friends with some of its leaders. **Her hopes soared**.

In 1903 a new social club was built in Salford, Manchester, where Labour Party members could meet and relax. The club was named in honour of Dr Richard Pankhurst, who had always been such a friend to the local poor. And Richard and Emmeline's daughter Sylvia, the budding artist, was asked to decorate the inside of the hall. With Emmeline's approval, she jumped at the chance. Then for months Sylvia beavered away, not asking for a penny in pay. She designed and painted huge panels covered with roses (which stood for love), apple trees (for knowledge), doves (for peace), corn (for plenty) and sunflowers (for hope). But just before the hall's official opening, **the bombshell dropped**.

It turned out that no women were going to be allowed into the social club!

Emmeline, who had been so pleased and proud, fell into despair. Surely this had to be a joke? But it wasn't. The Labour Party was turning out to be just as unfair and old-fashioned as the other two parties. Some Labour politicians were ready to stick up for women, but too many others were afraid that if they campaigned for female suffrage, they might make themselves unpopular with male voters. In this man-made world, with its man-made parties, there really wasn't much support for women.

But Emmeline didn't just despair. She didn't just get angry either. She'd always been a fighter and she always would be. Yes, this was a problem, but all problems had solutions – you just had to work out what they were.

Something Richard once said kept echoing in her head.

Why are women so patient? Why don't you force us to give you the vote? Why don't you scratch our eyes out!

Christabel too remembered her dad's words. She had already run out of patience.

Another generation of women cannot waste their lives begging for the vote. We must not lose any more time. We must act!

Then the solution came to Emmeline.

Facts were facts and rules were rules. But those facts and rules could be changed! It was time for women to act. Young women and older women together. Women of all classes. They would **fight and fight** until they got what they wanted, but they could not rely on men to help them – instead they would form a women's party!

On the roller-coaster ride of Emmeline Pankhurst's life, it was time for everyone to fasten their safety belts . . .

EMMELINE KICKS UP A FUSS

Women's Social and Political Union

That's what Emmeline decided to call her new party at its first meeting. There were nearly more words in the name than people in the room, but the number of members soon rocketed. And once they became more famous, people gave them a snappier nickname too. But that didn't happen for a couple of years, so you'll have to wait a few pages to find out what it was.

Yet even while Emmeline's Union was still tiny, she had **big, big plans**, and right from the start Emmeline believed that it would succeed. She always had total faith in herself and her projects.

GIRLPOWER IN ACTION

Emmeline's Union said men and women were equal. Therefore women should have just as many votes as men. It seemed an impossible goal, and from day one on 10th October 1903 there were some basic ground rules:

In Emmeline's view, women's protests had been polite for too long. It was all very well writing letter after letter to the newspapers, but letters were easy to ignore. There were other ways to get attention – pushier, more 'militant' ways. Emmeline egged her women on to heckle (interrupt) when top male politicians held their meetings, and even to badger them outside their own homes.

So that's what they did. It was **most unladylike** and really **quite shocking** – but it put the Union in the news, which was exactly where they wanted to be. Shouting at top men about women's suffrage could also be pretty good fun if you enjoyed that kind of thing, and Team Pankhurst most certainly did. Union members made Liberal politician Winston Churchill a particular target for their heckling. He hit back by saying he would not be 'henpecked' – then afterwards, wherever he went in Manchester, people cried out, **`Don't be henpecked, Winston!'**

No More Patient Babies

Meanwhile, Emmeline gave speech after speech for the cause. Thanks to her experience at places like Boggart Hole Clough, she'd become a really terrific public speaker, and she knew just how to reach out to audiences with her message . . .

You have two babies very hungry and wanting to be fed. One baby is a patient baby, and waits indefinitely until its mother is ready to feed it. The other baby is an impatient baby and cries lustily, screams and kicks and makes everybody unpleasant until it is fed.

Well, we know perfectly well which baby is attended to first. That is the whole history of politics . . . You have to make more noise than anybody else . . . You have to fill all the papers more than anybody else, in fact you have to be there all the time and see that they do not snow you under . . .

She travelled great distances to spread the word about the need for women's suffrage. But she didn't give up her day job as a registrar. Nor did she close down Emerson's. She couldn't afford to. She still **needed every penny** she could earn – and not just for her family. A lot of Emmeline's hard-earned money went into advertising forthcoming Union events, and hiring the halls where they were held and paying members' travel expenses. She sometimes had to sell artworks by Sylvia to cover her own train fares, while other Union members held fundraising jumble sales.

But whenever Emmeline stepped onto a stage, something magical happened. There she would stand – a small woman in a dress of pale purple or black, looking elegant but quite fragile – and people didn't know quite what to expect. She never used a microphone. She hardly ever glanced at any notes. She didn't stamp about or wave her arms. Yet as soon as she opened her mouth **she was mesmerizing** – no one could doubt how passionate she was. Or how much was at stake for her . . .

I would rather be a rebel than a slave. I would rather die than submit; and that is the spirit that animates this movement . . . I mean to be a voter in the land that gave me birth!

There were no big video screens to show close-ups of her face, but Emmeline somehow made people focus so hard on her, she could electrify them just by changing her expression. A famous writer called Rebecca West heard one of her speeches and wrote:

When she lifted up her hoarse, sweet voice, she was trembling like a reed. Only the reed was made of steel, and it was tremendous.

Emmeline was still nervy before each performance, but that just encouraged her to put in twice the amount of effort, and she went on inspiring audience after audience. Afterwards huge numbers of her listeners would rush to become Union members – and since each new member had to pay a fee, that helped with the funds. Some people also made generous gifts of money, and eventually Emmeline stopped having to unfasten her own purse to help pay for the whole campaign.

It's A Family Affair

Emmeline was the figurehead for the Union and its key speaker, but she wasn't the only Pankhurst to give speeches. Christabel, Sylvia and even Adela joined the movement. All three would set down soapboxes on village greens or outside factory gates, step up onto them, then **speak, speak, speak**. Team Pankhurst was back in business. Harry too was a keen supporter, although being a man he wasn't allowed to join the Union. Even for Emmeline's family there could be no exceptions. Here was one club where men could not call all the shots.

The three girls still followed their own studies. But all their spare moments were spent on militant Union work. Emmeline was thrilled to find that

Christabel was especially good at public speaking. Now, at long last, she'd discovered what she did best. When men showed up at the Union's meetings just to shout insults, Emmeline laughed as her quick-witted daughter answered them back.

Go home and do the washing!

My good man, don't you know that Monday is washing day and this is Thursday?

Wouldn't you like to be a man, miss?

Wouldn't you?

The Union went on holding meetings, and heckling and henpecking at other people's meetings. After a couple of years this made them quite well known, but still, they weren't really nationwide news and the Government wasn't taking them too seriously.

That bothered Emmeline. She longed for her message to be spread right across the country. The Union's demands were only fair and sensible, she thought. So if millions of people got to hear them, they would surely all be convinced – then they would make the Government bring in votes for women.

Somehow the Union needed more publicity, and

late in 1905 they managed to win that publicity. They really hit the jackpot. But this time it wasn't thanks to Emmeline.

CHRISTABEL TEACHES EMMELINE A LESSON

On the evening of 13th October there was going to be a big meeting at Manchester's Free Trade Hall with a politician called Sir Edward Grey making a speech. As Christabel left the house for the hall, accompanied by a young working-class Union member called Annie Kenney, she said with a mischievous smile to her mum, 'We shall sleep in prison tonight!'

That made Emmeline anxious enough, but she was staggered when she learned hours later exactly what her daughter had meant. Suffrage was not on the meeting's agenda, but Christabel and Annie kept heckling Sir Edward about votes for women. This set off such an uproar that some stewards, there to keep order, grabbed the two women and dragged them roughly out of the hall. Outside the pair then did something so utterly 'unladylike', it took everyone's breath away. And they did it absolutely on purpose. **They spat at a policeman**!

PTOO

73

The girls knew this would get them arrested – and when they refused to pay a fine, there was nothing else for it: they really would have to go to jail.

Emmeline was horrified. The idea of two defenceless young women under lock and key! She pleaded with them both to let her pay the fine and take them home. 'Mother,' Christabel replied, 'if you pay my fine I'll never go home.'

Unlike Emmeline at Boggart Hole Clough all those years before, Christabel and Annie were actually taken off to Manchester's Strangeways Prison and put in the cells. And if workhouses were bad, prisons at that time were even worse.

Christabel and Annie were inside for only a few days. But when they came out, the newspapers were full of their story, and people all round the country were talking about them.

By now Emmeline realized how clever Christabel had been. She herself wouldn't have chosen this way to get people to sit up and take notice – but there was no denying its impact. Everyone was shocked that women could be treated so harshly. After that, other young Union members copied Christabel's example. They 'obstructed' the police then refused to pay their fines, so they too had to serve time in prison – and the police were often **none too gentle** when arresting them. It was all fantastic publicity for the Union. Emmeline was so grateful to Christabel for that.

They sound like chirping sparrows, put them in a cage, I say!

But these women aren't really doing anything wrong. All they want is the right to vote!

What's In A Name?

From then on, the press couldn't get enough of Emmeline, Christabel and the Union. Papers like the brand new *Daily Mirror*, splashed with photos of posh ladies **getting up to no good** in public, flew off the news stands.

The *Daily Mail* even came up with a new name for them – one that was a bit less of a mouthful than 'Members of the Women's Social and Political Union'. You may already know that a woman with dark brown hair is a 'brunette' and a woman who works in a cinema is an 'usherette'. So, because the Union protestors were all women, and they were all campaigning for suffrage the *Daily Mail* called them:

SUFFRAGETTES!

Even if it was meant as a bit of an insult, the Union members didn't care – the more people talked about 'suffragettes', the more coverage their cause got. Soon the Union was even printing up a newspaper of its own. Emmeline was delighted. *Votes for Women* started out as a monthly but it quickly became a weekly. Each issue cost just one penny and in its heyday it sold a whopping 22,000 copies a week.

The bigger the Union became, the more Emmeline

relied on other important organizers, including Sylvia and Adela. But if anyone was her main helper it was Christabel, who had by now managed to get herself a first-class law degree.

Sometimes it was hard to know quite who was in charge – mum or daughter – and as the two grew ever closer, Sylvia and Adela started to feel a bit left out.

More and more paying members joined, so the money rolled in. Non-members made big donations too. Nearly £3,000 poured in between March 1906 and February 1907. The next year this leaped to £7,545, and the year after that it increased to a whopping £21,213. Money was worth more then too. Just £1 could keep a family going for a whole week. This meant there was more than enough cash to pay Emmeline's expenses. So, taking a deep breath, she gave up all her other working commitments to devote herself to the Union.

Now it was **all or nothing** for the cause. From event to event she whirled around Britain, staying in hotels or in the spare rooms of wealthy suffragette supporters. But in early 1908 she had to stay put for over a month in just one place: Holloway, London's famous prison for women.

Emmeline Steps Into The Unknown

Plenty of young suffragette militants had been arrested then sent to prison for refusing to pay their fines. In January and February of 1907 alone, **130 women were sent to prison**. Why? Because they'd tried to present a petition to the Prime Minister – perfectly peacefully, no spitting involved at all.

Clearly the Government was beginning to see the suffragettes as more than just 'chirping sparrows'. This set Emmeline thinking: each imprisonment won more publicity for her movement. But how much more publicity might there be if she herself went behind bars? After discussing this possibility with her right-hand women, Emmeline – fearless as ever – decided to find out.

An old law made it illegal for more than 10 people to take a petition to Parliament, so she made it known that on Valentine's Day 1908 she planned to do just that, walking with 12 other women to the House of Commons.

It wasn't that easy for Emmeline to walk. In fact she had to limp all the way – just a month before, she had badly hurt her ankle trying to get away from a gang of male thugs at a meeting in Devon. She'd had to take cover in a local shop after being pelted with their clay missiles, rotten eggs and snowballs packed with stones.

A huge crowd turned out to see what happened outside Parliament. In one hand Emmeline held a rolled-up petition demanding women's suffrage, in the other a small bunch of lilies of the valley. And even though this was to be a completely peaceful demonstration, the police were out in force, on foot and on horseback. 'You might have supposed,' Emmeline later wrote, 'that instead of thirteen women, one of them lame, walking quietly along, the town was in the hands of **an armed mob**.'

At the entrance to Parliament Square, two large policemen grabbed her on either side and told her she was under arrest. No way of course was she going to pay a fine. So it was that Emmeline Pankhurst was sentenced to six weeks in Holloway.

Her father had not had his golden daughter 'finished' for this. If he'd still been alive, the shame would have probably finished *him* off. Emmeline herself had no time for shame. If she had to spend six weeks in a Holloway cell for her suffragette beliefs, then **she would do it gladly**. And as she well knew from Christabel's experience the previous year, the newspapers would make sure it made all the headlines.

Holloway Hell

Emmeline never forgot her first time inside. She may have got off lightly compared to more regular, lower-class offenders but it was still pretty gruesome.

The whole place stank. And somehow it was both the stuffiest and the draughtiest building I have ever been in.

She'd never in her life been made to wear such clothes: stained underwear, rough brown-and-red striped stockings, a dress with arrows on it. Her cell was tiny, with a window too high to look out of. The mattress and pillows on her narrow bed were rock hard. On a shelf in the corner stood a black tin pot that her food was slopped into and a wooden spoon to eat it with. Leaning against a wall were a tin basin for washing, and a tin potty with a lid.

Emmeline soon got sick, so she had to be moved for a while to the prison hospital. There, in the middle of one night, she was woken by another prisoner's screams. In that most gruesome of places, the poor woman was **having a baby**!

The iron door to Emmeline's cell was studded with nails. At its centre was a rectangular hole filled with glass and covered by an iron flap. Female warders on the other side of the door could lift the flap to spy on their prisoner. Emmeline made sure they were surprised by what they saw. Whether she happened to be in Seedley Cottage or a stinking prison, she was never one for idling away her time. So she'd spend long hours sitting on her bed sewing or knitting. She also asked for writing materials, and when she was given chalk and a slate, she wrote down all the French poems she could remember.

Maybe the prison officers thought she would crack under the pressure. Maybe now and then – shivering in her ugly prison clothes, far from all her loved ones – Emmeline thought she might too. But she was **tough and brave** and she never showed a moment's **fear or weakness.** Some might have said she took her punishment like a man.

NO! I took it like a WOMAN!

82

A Rousing Reception

Meanwhile outside in the free world, the suffragettes had cranked up their constant fundraising drive a few notches. Some members stopped buying luxuries like coffee or cocoa and handed the money to the Union instead; some sold jewellery or lace, others made street collections. The total raised was to be announced at a meeting in London's Royal Albert Hall on 19th March 1908, the day before Emmeline was due to be released from prison.

When the evening came, a crowd of thousands filled the hall. Christabel greeted them from a platform beside an empty chair that had Emmeline's name on it. Thanks to some extra-large donations, they had raised a full £7,000 pounds **in just one week**! Loud cheers greeted that news, but Christabel had an even bigger surprise up her sleeve. She teased the crowd by saying that someone had just arrived, someone they might be very pleased to see . . .

Everyone caught their breath. They could hardly believe their eyes when a pale, visibly weary Emmeline quietly walked across the stage to take her seat. She'd been released a day early!

A great cry went up from the women. They sprang from their seats and stretched out their hands towards her as if she were a goddess. It was some time before she was able to see them through her tears, and the storm of emotion shook her to the core. After all that had happened in Holloway, most women wouldn't have dreamed of addressing an audience. But from deep inside herself Emmeline Pankhurst summoned the energy to keep the entire hall spellbound:

Looking round on the muddles that men have made . . . I say men have had the control of these things long enough, and no woman with any spark of womanliness in her will consent to let this state of things go on any longer. We are tired of it.
They said, 'You will never rouse women.' Well, we have done what they thought and what they hoped to be impossible.
We women are roused!

Her words brought the house down.

That night the suffragettes believed anything was possible. Emmeline felt convinced that her party's militant campaign was about to reach a glorious end. Victory really did seem to be in sight.

But for all her faith, **she was wrong**.

Things were about to get worse, much worse, for the suffragettes . . .

6   Emmeline Gets Frustrated

By the summer of 1908 Emmeline and the
suffragettes could hardly have been more famous.
They were front-page news not just in Britain
but overseas as well.

Everything was going to plan. The Union was
getting masses of backing from men and women alike,
and a number of MPs were even supporting their
cause. But these MPs were not part of the country's

Liberal Government, and if the Government didn't put forward a new law giving the vote to women, nothing could change. So Emmeline decided this Government needed to be shown just how much support there was for women's suffrage. On 21st June 1908 the suffragettes organized their biggest-ever rally in London's Hyde Park, and **spent over £1000** (roughly £110,000 today) just to advertise it . . .

'A Vast Garden In Full Bloom'

The size of the crowd was awesome. 'It is probable,' said the *Daily Express*, 'that so many people never before stood in one square mass anywhere in England.'

It lifted Emmeline's heart to look out from her platform at that vast ocean of people in the brilliant sunshine. There were maybe half a million of them – and she was so proud that not one was doing anything that might get them arrested! To think she had founded the Union five years before with just a handful of women – now this.

It was almost too much for her to take in: the seven great processions that had converged on the park, the people from all over Britain who'd travelled in on special trains, the brass bands playing, the **700 banners** fluttering in the light breeze, the

19 other platforms from which 80 different speakers gave passionate speeches for the Union's cause, the stalls selling 'Votes for Women' button badges and brooches . . .

It was a gay and beautiful as well as an awe-inspiring spectacle, for the white gowns and flower-trimmed hats of the women, against the background of ancient trees, gave the park the appearance of a vast garden in full bloom.

WOMEN DEMAND VOTE!

DEEDS NOT WORDS

W.S.P.U

W.S.P.U

The whole city seemed to have turned suffragette, since so many in the crowd wore the Union's new 'official' colours of white for purity, green for hope, and purple for dignity. And it truly was a day of hope and dignity. It was the dignity that moved Emmeline the most. In the past she and her members had often been ridiculed and insulted, but **scarcely anyone** was making fun of them at this gigantic, blissfully peaceful demonstration. It was as if the world had finally come to its senses and realized women had to be treated as equal to men. Prime Minister Herbert Asquith couldn't fail to see there was now only one way forward. So at the day's end a special messenger was sent to him with a simple message from all the women:

POST OFFICE TELEGRAM

STAMP

3M

GRANT VOTES TO US WITHOUT DELAY!

So Near And Yet So Far

Within two days, they got their answer. The Prime Minister had never been a friend to the suffragettes. In fact Mr Asquith had often been **quite rude** about them and he still saw no reason to rush through a new law. In his view, the suffragettes didn't have all that much support. Emmeline and her Union would just have to go on being patient, he said. The Government had more urgent business to be getting on with.

First Emmeline felt crushed, then the fury kicked in. All that hard work, all that battling for the cause, all those imprisonments, all that hope (because Emmeline's kind of protest and anger had to be based on hope) – and still the Union seemed to be getting nowhere. She had been so keen to win the vote for women by peaceful means, but here was a wake-up call she could not ignore. Now it was clear for all to see: purely peaceful protest wasn't working.

Either we had to give up our agitation altogether . . . or else we must act, and go on acting, until the selfishness and obstinacy of the Government was broken down, or the Government destroyed.

And when she spoke of acting, she wasn't thinking about taking 'ladylike' actions . . .

But in a way Mr Asquith had been right. Not everyone who turned up at suffragette events was a supporter. Many came just because they were curious about these unusual women. Some – mainly men – came to **have a bit of fun**. They set live mice free among the audiences.

Small boys came armed with **peashooters and pockets full of dried peas.** Bigger ones threw rotten eggs, oranges and fish at the speakers, who did their level best to go on speaking (but a hail of dried peas really stung).

At the same time, the non-militant suffragists were still campaigning away as patiently as ever. In 1907, deciding that this less militant approach might in fact work better, some leading suffragette organizers left the Union. They thought Emmeline had become more interested in getting support from well-heeled ladies than from lower-class women. (Which wasn't really true, but those posh ladies in their rustling silks and satins did have more funds to contribute to the cause.) The leavers also found the Union's leader to be quite – how to put this? – **bossy.**

Bossy? ME?!

Emmeline wasn't sorry to see them go. The Union was a suffrage army, she declared, yet it was an army of volunteers, so no one had to stay part of it if they didn't want to. If they did stay, however, they had to toe the Pankhurst line. As Emmeline put it:

When going into battle, a general does not take a vote of his soldiers to see if they approve of his plans. They are there to obey his orders. That is how the WSPU has been run and that is how it will continue to be run.

Meanwhile, for the likes of Emmeline and Christabel – enraged by the Liberal Government rejecting their demands – there were plenty more policemen to obstruct, plenty more prison cells to spend a few nights in. To them, this really was turning into a kind of combat, although Emmeline herself still wouldn't have hurt a fly – just the thought of violence **made her shudder**. But a small handful of women in her 'army' weren't in two minds at all. They went right ahead and took the law into their own hands.

WOMEN ON THE WARPATH

In 1909, out of sheer frustration, a group of suffragettes smashed the windows of some Government offices in London. Emmeline didn't tell them to do this. But she didn't tell them off for doing it either.

Emmeline hated violence with a passion, but all the years of peaceful militancy had not brought a result. She even turned a blind eye when in Birmingham two suffragettes climbed onto a roof, loosened some slates with axes and **hurled them down** at the Prime Minister's car (taking great care not to hit either him or his driver).

Mr Asquith had to have a police escort wherever he went. He even had to watch out for suffragette ambushes when he was relaxing on the golf course.

This all seemed outrageous to some politicians, and to some members of the public, who took to calling these unladylike protestors 'hooligans'.

But if Emmeline thought this might encourage her 'arch enemy' to give women the vote, she was wrong. In his way Mr Asquith was quite as stubborn and determined as she was, and his wife gave him total support.

As the fight for equal rights for women began to shape up, some men supported the women, while **some women backed the men**. Quite confusing!

FEEDING FRENZY

As more suffragettes turned to violence, more were arrested and jailed. Some even padlocked themselves to the railings of Government buildings. This gave them a chance to make long political speeches to passers-by during the time it took for the police to cut them out of their chains – otherwise they'd have been arrested at once!

But even in prison there were ways for them to cause trouble, and to get out quicker. A suffragette called Marion Dunlop hit on the bright idea of refusing to eat the meals the Holloway warders gave her.

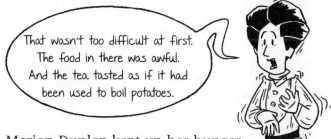

That wasn't too difficult at first. The food in there was awful. And the tea tasted as if it had been used to boil potatoes.

Marion Dunlop kept up her hunger strike. **She ate and drank nothing for 91 hours** – that's nearly four days – until in the end she had to be set free. The last thing the prison officers or the Government wanted was for a suffragette to die in jail: the newspapers would never have stopped going on about that. Many other copycat suffragettes then said 'No to Nourishment' too – and fasting quickly became a trademark Union protest. Again Emmeline did not speak out against what they were doing, but she was horrified by the next piece of news.

Some of our women were being forced to eat – mainly by other women!

If you're squeamish, you should probably skip the next bit. Here is suffragette Mary Leigh's account of how eight female prison warders and two male doctors got food into her:

The wardresses forced me on to the bed and the two doctors came in with them, and while I was held down, a nasal tube was inserted. It is two yards long with a funnel at the end – there is a glass junction in the middle to see if the liquid is passing . . . They must have seen my pain, for the other doctor interfered (the matron and two of the wardresses were in tears) and they stopped and resorted to feeding me by the spoon . . . the sensation is most painful – the drums of the ear seem to be bursting, a horrible pain in the throat and the breast. The tube is pushed down twenty inches . . . about a pint of milk, sometimes egg and milk, are used . . . before and after they test my heart and make a lot of examination. The after-effects are a feeling of faintness, a sense of great pain in the diaphragm or breast bone, in the nose and the ears . . . I was very sick on the first occasion after the tube was withdrawn.

M. L.

The women didn't have to put up with it just once. Late in 1909 suffragette Charlotte Marsh was let out of Winson Green prison in Birmingham after she'd been force-fed **a mind-boggling 139 times** in three months.

Prison officials, stewards and policemen all seemed to have no problem roughly manhandling suffragettes. Their cruelty staggered Emmeline. Why should women be treated in this inhuman way – and just because they wanted the vote? Plenty of newspaper readers across the country agreed with her. Shocking though the 'hooliganism' of the militant suffragettes was, they didn't deserve this violent response.

Emmeline Makes A Mercy Dash

In the midst of the mayhem, Emmeline continued to tour the country, making every effort to convert as many people as possible to the cause. She had a special suffragette motor car to take her to her many appointments. Cars were still a rare sight on the roads, and since Emmeline hadn't learned to drive, the Union had to employ a number of female chauffeurs, including a young woman called Aileen Preston. Aileen's well-to-do family were horrified when they heard she was driving 'that dreadful woman' – Emmeline – all over the country.

Audiences far beyond Britain's shores were also eager to hear Emmeline speak. Women in America (and in most other countries) had no more right to vote than their British sisters, and Emmeline always thought **big, big, big.** Once the suffragettes had won their fight in Britain, she believed, it would be easier for women all over the world to win their fight too. So she decided to make a whirlwind tour of American cities to encourage and inform American women protestors – and some of the fees for her speeches could help boost campaign funds back at home.

But towards the end of 1909, there was a more personal need for Emmeline to raise cash too. Her son Harry had never been very healthy. Now, at the age of 19, he'd fallen ill with the serious disease poliomyelitis.

The British National Health Service didn't exist back then and doctors didn't treat you for free. Harry could no longer work and he had no savings either, so a portion of Emmeline's speech fees could also be put towards paying for his medical care. That was the situation Emmeline left behind as she set sail across the Atlantic – relieved that she could get some well-deserved downtime on the long voyages there and back.

A Third Hit To The Heart

While Sylvia and Christabel looked after Harry, Emmeline wowed American audiences.

Wherever she travelled, thousands cheered her on. Reporters called her '**the most talked-about woman in the world**' and 'the best-loved and best-hated woman in England'. It was the first time she'd ever travelled outside Europe, and it touched her heart to find such support and sympathy. But all too soon, Emmeline's whirlwind tour was over, and she had to return to her struggles at home.

She brought back a sack-load of money. But one look at Harry wiped any smile off Emmeline's face. To her horror, her son's condition had worsened in her absence. He'd been paralysed by his illness. All the money in the world couldn't have helped him now – **there really was no cure**. And early in 1910, surrounded by his loving family, the youngest Pankhurst died.

Emmeline had lost her dear son Frank as a small child, then she'd lost her soulmate Richard, and now a third male member of her family – the one who had always been 'her baby' – had been taken. The pain was too great. At Harry's funeral she looked to the other mourners as if she might break apart. But that very evening she was due to make a speech in Manchester, and she wasn't about to let anyone down. Just as planned, she stepped out on stage and electrified over 5,000 people with her words:

Surely every mother here knows that I would rather be quiet tonight, by my own fireside with my sad thoughts, and it is only a sense of my great responsibility and duty in this campaign that has urged me to appear . . .

The whirlwind had to go on. Being busy was Emmeline's way of living with her grief. Or maybe it was her way of blocking it out.

Fresh Hope And A 'Truce'

Now Emmeline wasn't the only one with her hands full.

Prime Minister Asquith was very busy too. In some ways his Government actually was making life better and safer for the British people: it had started to pay old-age pensions to senior citizens, and was trying to bring in free school meals. But there was **serious trouble** of a different sort brewing across the English Channel. There hadn't been a full-scale

European war since the 1870s, but people sensed another coming. So the British Government was doing all it could to help keep the peace – whilst getting ready to fight if war should break out.

MPs were still discussing votes for women, though. There was even talk of a new female suffrage law. A special committee was set up in Parliament so that the whole thing could be debated. Round and round the arguing went. Should suffrage be given to **all women**? Or should it just go to women who didn't have husbands? (Because husbands might bully their wives over how they voted – and so more or less get two votes for themselves.) The Liberals were afraid most women would vote Conservative. The Conservatives feared most women would vote Liberal. Even outside Parliament people worried about change.

The debate went on in Parliament through most of 1910, and then 1911 too.

But at least the suffragettes now **had a chance** of getting what they wanted. So Emmeline and the rest of the Union's high command called a 'truce' with the Government – not for ever, just while there was still hope of a new law coming in. In the meantime the suffragettes still held peaceful protest meetings, demonstrations and parades. They carried on selling souvenirs too to keep campaign cash rolling in.

Get your official merchandise here! Celebrity suffragette scarves and postcards! Everything in this year's colours – purple, green and white. So much smarter than last year's colours (green, white and purple).

Trinkets & Memorabilia

But though Emmeline tried to get her suffragette 'troops' to stick to the truce, they didn't always obey. Many went on being imprisoned for obstructing the police, and still there were hunger strikes and force-feeding. The risks for the women involved were made terribly clear to Emmeline at the end of 1910. Her favourite sister Mary, her children's 'deputy mother', was one of the suffragettes sent to prison and force-fed. Released three days before Christmas, she **collapsed and died** of a burst blood vessel in her brain on Christmas Day itself. She was only 48 years old. Emmeline had no doubt that force-feeding had hastened her death.

'She is the first to die,' she wrote in a sombre letter. 'How many must follow?'

Putting The 'RAGE' Into 'SuffRAGEttes'

Late in 1911 Emmeline crossed the Atlantic again to make some speeches. Although she was fretting about the discussions in Parliament, she still made a triumphant tour of the USA and Canada. It was good for her to feel loved and wanted, because back at home increasing numbers of men, and women, were questioning her Union's militant ways.

They also questioned why Emmeline had gone off on her travels again. Was it to raise funds for the suffragette campaign, or to raise college fees for Adela? The youngest Pankhurst girl had stopped teaching to help run the Union, but her health had suffered, so now Emmeline wanted her to be a student. And just who was paying for Emmeline's trips anyway? No one could prove it, but at times it looked like the Pankhursts were using suffragette funds for their own private ends.

Emmeline tried not to let the critics get her down. All that really mattered was what happened in Parliament. Day by day the tension grew as she waited to hear what the politicians back in London had decided. And right at the end of the year, in the American city of Minneapolis, a telegram from England arrived for her.

The news was about as bad as it could be:

POST OFFICE
TELEGRAM

STAMP
3M

VOTES FOR WOMEN PUT OFF YET AGAIN.
BUT 4 MILLION MORE MEN TO GET VOTES.

Would you believe it!

After the truce, Emmeline saw this as a complete betrayal. She thought she might **burst with rage**, and her loyal suffragettes very nearly did. On a single night in London, **220 women were arrested** for using stones and hammers to break windows. Not just the windows of Government buildings – they also smashed the windows of post offices, big West End stores (where Emmeline herself still loved to window-shop and kept an eye out for sales) and the headquarters of two national newspapers. A suffragette called Emily Davison took things one step further. She stuffed burning rags into pillar boxes full of letters and **set them on fire**.

With Emmeline far away across the ocean, things were starting to get out of hand. But the big question on everyone's mind – and in every feverish newspaper report – was this: when Emmeline got home, what new orders would she give? Would she try to calm her troops down – or would she go for all-out attack?

7   EMMELINE THROWS HER FIRST STONE

Late on a February day in 1912, not far outside of London, two posh ladies and a dog emerged from a country cottage. They looked as if they were up to no good. After making sure no one else was around, they gathered a pile of stones. Then the first woman, who was a talented composer of music called Ethel Smyth, pointed at a nearby fir tree. This would be their target. The other woman – Emmeline – nodded.

Ethel hurled stone after stone at the tree, giving a masterclass in how to aim and throw. Emmeline thought it looked dead easy, so up she stepped to take her turn.

She lifted her arm and let fly with all her strength – but her own stone didn't go anywhere near the tree. Instead it flew backwards, landing inches from the startled dog.

The tree Emmeline! Throw it at the tree!

Yiiipe

Furious with herself, Emmeline tried again. And again. And again. But all her throws completely missed the target, and with each new failure she got angrier and angrier until finally, thankfully, a dull thwack sounded in the gloom. She'd made a direct hit!

She beamed with such pride that Ethel **burst out laughing**.

But Emmeline narrowed her eyes at Ethel. She hadn't come to her friend's cottage to learn this new skill just for fun. In fact, the most serious and frightening time of her whole roller-coaster life was about to begin. She'd made up her mind that the Union must fight. Windows would be broken (especially by more accurate suffragettes). Things would be set on fire. In the end – Emmeline hoped – the Government would let women have the vote just to keep them quiet!

Ladies and Gentlemen, we are firmly convinced . . . that this is the only way to get women's suffrage. We shall never get this question settled until we make it intolerable for most people in this country, until we make the question such a nuisance you will all want to find a way of getting rid of the nuisance!

What's In That Woman's Handbag?

Several days later, back in London, Emmeline led a small group of suffragettes to a different and rather more important target. At 5.30 in the evening she and two other Union members got out of a taxi near 10 Downing Street, Prime Minister Asquith's home.

Emmeline had it all worked out. She would hurl stones at the Prime Minister's windows. Then she would be arrested and thrown into prison, where she'd starve herself until she was so **dangerously weak** that they would have to set her free.

On that first evening in 1912, everything went perfectly to plan.

What Emmeline could not have known was that this was just the start. The campaign of violence she now led would last for almost three years, and she would keep being arrested, keep going on hunger strike.

She never did anything harmful herself. Despite Ethel Smyth's expert training, Emmeline's stones even missed the Prime Minister's windows. But as the ringleader of much wilder suffragettes, she had to keep taking the rap for what they did. They were, after all, carrying out her wishes. And many of them were ready to shift heaven and earth for their leader. 'While we admired Christabel,' one suffragette recalled in her old age, 'we loved Mrs Pankhurst.'

They would cut the message 'Votes for Women' into golf courses where wealthy politicians enjoyed their time off, then pour acid onto the greens to make them impossible to play on. They broke the windows of clubs where wealthy politicians met to eat and chat. They destroyed the refreshment house in Regent's Park, London, and slashed priceless paintings in Manchester and London art galleries. Even the orchid house at London's Kew Gardens was attacked.

At one point the *Daily Mail* worked out that the suffragettes had done nearly **half a million pounds' worth of damage**.

Well, looks like golf is out of the question. Shall we get lunch?

VOTES FOR WOMEN

Now everyone threw worried glances at any well-dressed woman out in public on her own. (Women who couldn't afford nice clothes wouldn't have been able to get time off work.) She might look harmless. But **what was in that handbag** of hers?

During her prison stays, Emmeline at least avoided being force-fed when she went without food. The prison doctors were worried that, at her age, her heart might stop. But the force-feeding of younger suffragettes went on all around her.

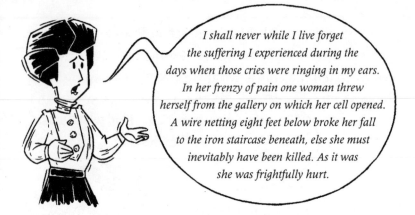

I shall never while I live forget the suffering I experienced during the days when those cries were ringing in my ears. In her frenzy of pain one woman threw herself from the gallery on which her cell opened. A wire netting eight feet below broke her fall to the iron staircase beneath, else she must inevitably have been killed. As it was she was frightfully hurt.

Emmeline thought it was **scandalous** to put women through this. Suffragette supporters who read about it in their newspapers thought so too. But many of them also wondered if all this upheaval was actually getting women any closer to the vote.

Playing Cat And Mouse

In April 1913, Emmeline got her longest prison sentence yet. Three years – for plotting to blow up the house of a Government minister. That sounds worse than it really was: the house was still being built and the minister was miles away at the time. The Union made a point of attacking only empty buildings, usually at night. 'Mrs Pankhurst gave us strict instructions . . . ' wrote one of her followers later. 'There was not a cat or a canary to be killed.'

Even so, **a bomb had been set off**, and that was against the law. For years Emmeline had been trying to tell the courts what was really happening . . .

We are here, not because we are law-breakers; we are here in our efforts to become law-makers.

But the courts didn't listen – and once again Emmeline had to go down.

But no way could she serve three years in prison without food or drink, and she couldn't be force-fed, so the Government came up with a cunning plan. It rushed out a new law (it could do that if it wanted). This law said a hunger striker might be set free if the prison doctors thought her life was in danger, but once she was fit and healthy again she would have to go back to jail. While she was recovering too, she'd have to let the police know exactly where she was.

People called this new law **'The Cat and Mouse Act'**, because the Government was like a cat playing around with its prey – the hunger-striking 'mice'. But it did mean fewer suffragettes now had to be force-fed.

The Scars Of Battle

As a result of the Act, Emmeline yo-yoed in and out of prison more than ever – starving and recovering, starving and recovering. This would have weakened even a fit young person's body. But Emmeline was a woman in her mid-50s, so she really suffered. Here is how she described what happened when she refused water, which she said was much worse than going without food:

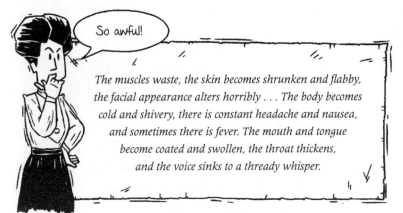

So awful!

The muscles waste, the skin becomes shrunken and flabby, the facial appearance alters horribly . . . The body becomes cold and shivery, there is constant headache and nausea, and sometimes there is fever. The mouth and tongue become coated and swollen, the throat thickens, and the voice sinks to a thready whisper.

In prison she suffered from jaundice, and never really shook it off for the rest of her life. A nurse called Catherine Pine looked after her each time she came out of prison, but it took longer and longer for Emmeline to get back to full health. Her many hunger strikes were leaving her **weak, depressed, dizzy and exhausted**.

Yet still she soldiered on. Long ago, her nickname had been The Dictionary, with so many words at the tips of her fingers. Now only three words mattered to her: **Votes!...For!...Women!**

THE SUFFRAGETTE

FIGHT! FIGHT! FIGHT!

We are fighting for a time when every little girl born into the world will have an equal chance with her brothers! We are soldiers in a holy war. And we mean to go on until victory is won!

Often Emmeline didn't return to prison when she was meant to. Detectives came to rearrest her, but she would dress up a friend to look like her. Then the friend would be arrested, and Emmeline could make her getaway to do a bit more organizing. One time she even got as far as the USA, and made another whirlwind tour.

For help with these decoy operations, and to protect her from police attacks, Emmeline now had a **special bodyguard** of up to 30 women volunteers, trained in the martial art of ju-jitsu.

They looked normal enough (though they were all pretty well-built), but under their dresses they packed **wooden clubs** tied to their waists, and **layers of cardboard** to cushion the blows from policemen's truncheons.

Then one suffragette did something that made front-page news all over the world . . .

The Derby Day Calamity

It all happened so fast, no one could be sure what was going on.

It was 4th June 1913, the day of the world-famous Derby horse race at Epsom racecourse. As the horses thundered past the spectators at full pelt, a woman ducked under the barrier and onto the track. Four seconds later a terrified horse **smashed into her**. Both she and the jockey were sent flying – but only the horse and jockey survived. The dead woman was a suffragette, Emily Davison: the pillar-box burner, who had gone on **seven hunger strikes and been force-fed 49 times**.

Even today we can't know for certain what this lone suffragette was up to. Some said she had planned to sacrifice her life for the Union cause. Others claimed she just wanted to pin a flag with the Union colours to the passing horse, which happened to belong to the king.

Five thousand women marched at Emily's funeral. They did not include Emmeline – when she tried to travel to it, she was arrested under the Cat and Mouse Act. She hadn't wanted any Union member to lose her life, but she called Emily 'one of our bravest soldiers', and added that by dying she had drawn attention to the 'great struggle for the emancipation [or setting free] of women'.

They say no publicity is bad publicity, but many people who saw the news film of Emily's death lost sympathy for the cause. If that jockey had died, it would have looked like murder. People seriously questioned whether this was the best way to get the suffrage law changed. Besides, men were supposed to be the savage ones, women were meant to be showing them how to raise their game.

Even within Emmeline's army, deep doubts set in as 1913 wore on. The Cat and Mouse Act seemed to be succeeding. Hunger strikers were offered a deal before they were released to get well again: if they swore to do no more damage, they wouldn't be rearrested. It was **pretty cruel** to tempt very sick women to give up their cause or else risk death, but some took this chance to opt out.

Others, who hadn't even been to prison, chose to leave the Union too, turned off by all the aggressive action. Emmeline still didn't wish harm to anyone on either side of the war, but she saw no reason to make the Union's protests any less violent.

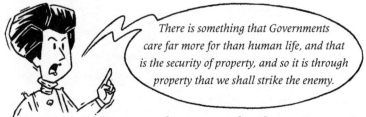

There is something that Governments care far more for than human life, and that is the security of property, and so it is through property that we shall strike the enemy.

In some ways, Emmeline's own battle tactics were getting wilder. In 1914 she led 100 women in a march on Buckingham Palace. If the Government wouldn't listen to her demands for women's suffrage, then perhaps the new king might.

But George V was still miffed by the attack on his horse at the Derby and he refused to meet the marchers. They pressed on anyway to the palace, with the police treating them as badly as ever along the route. Then, amid the chaos, Emmeline tiptoed unseen towards the palace gates. She planned to **duck inside** and go in search of the king. But at the last moment a burly police inspector lifted her right off the ground in a painful bear hug and she was carted back to prison.

FAMILY FALL-OUT

Emmeline did love being in the limelight. There was seldom a dull moment in her life, which was exactly how she liked it. Maybe, though, her life had become a bit too exciting. With all the violence and 'man-hating', she risked losing touch with many of the people she'd started off fighting for. And through all the ups and downs of her campaign, she never for a moment stopped feeling dreadfully lonely without her Richard. But from early 1912, Emmeline's lost husband wasn't the only family member she was missing. There were no two ways about it: **Team Pankhurst was falling apart**.

With Emmeline still in the thick of things in Britain, Christabel had taken herself off to France. She lived there in a fair amount of luxury, but continued to give out orders, which the suffragettes back home grumbled about but followed.

Meanwhile Sylvia and Adela found it so hard to accept the tactics of Emmeline and Christabel, they **left the Union altogether**, to fight for women's rights in their own ways.

The Calm Before The Biggest Storm

By the summer of 1914 the suffragettes and the Government seemed deadlocked, with neither side prepared to give way. As the Union lost popularity, even Emmeline must have wondered in her heart of hearts how much longer her army could keep up the fight.

Meanwhile she'd still served only six weeks of her three-year prison sentence and in July she was released from Holloway after yet another hunger strike. **She looked like a ghost** of her old self, and had some worrying pains around her heart. So instead of recovering at home then going back to prison, she slipped out of the country to join Christabel and her friend Ethel at the French seaside town of St Malo.

The other two women were helping Emmeline to get her strength back there when dreadful news arrived. This time there was no need for a telegram. To cries of shock and dismay, the local mayor made an announcement . . .

We are at war!

8 EMMELINE FORGIVES AND FORGETS

The news would mark a turning point not just in Emmeline's life, but in human history. France had declared war on Germany. Soon Britain would join in on the side of the French. World War I had begun.

At first Emmeline wasn't sure how this would affect her own war, but like almost everyone else in the autumn of 1914, she thought the conflict would be short, sharp and over by Christmas. If only women had been in charge, she suggested with a long-suffering sigh, there wouldn't have been any stupid war at all.

But the war was not short and sharp. It would drag on for four long years and almost 20 million people would lose their lives. By the end of 1914 it was already clear that **something truly horrific was happening.** This was a whole new world, and finally it changed Emmeline's way of thinking . . .

'FOR KING, FOR COUNTRY, FOR FREEDOM!'

Emmeline longed for the women of Britain to be free, but if the Germans invaded Britain there would be no country for women to be free in. It was all very tricky. While Emmeline chewed this over, the Government offered the suffragettes another truce – just until the war was over. Emmeline hummed and hawed about that, and in the end she said . . . yes.

After 11 years of struggle, the jailbirds were all set free. For the time being there would be no more protest of any kind whatever, no more prison sentences, no more Cat and Mouse. On the British home-front at least, peace was declared. So without the project she had given her life to, Emmeline suddenly had a lot of free time on her hands, but she didn't intend to stay at home twiddling her thumbs.

For one thing, she still didn't actually have a home of her own; for another, fighting was now in her blood. In those times, unlike today, only men got to serve as actual soldiers – and from early 1916 a new law said all able-bodied men aged 18 to 41 had to fight, or else risk execution (so though women used to have a hard time of it, men didn't have it all their own way either). Women were seen as 'weaker vessels' than men, so they were just expected to 'keep the home fires burning'. Which really wasn't enough for a woman who liked to think as big as Emmeline.

Making speeches was what she did best, and now she devoted all her public-speaking skills to making sure the war was won. With all the passion she'd once put into women's suffrage, **she spoke at rally after rally**, urging men to head off to the war, before that law of 1916 gave them no choice in the matter.

She campaigned too, with other suffragettes, for women to step into the jobs the men left behind them.

Soon women were serving their country as clerks and secretaries, in banks and businesses, as plumbers and window cleaners,

Right let's clean up this mess.

A woman driver? I'd rather walk!

Don't be so old-fashioned!

bus conductors and sometimes drivers. Hardly any of these jobs had ever been done by women before. They also got to stoke furnaces, unload coal wagons and build ships.

They even worked in factories where weapons and war equipment were made – *and* they were **promised the same pay** as male factory workers!

But how do you fire it?

It's for cooking, you idiot! Our soldiers have to eat.

Maybe this would all have happened anyway, without Emmeline campaigning for it. But whatever Emmeline chose to make speeches about, it was hard for people not to listen. She had a unique way of making people think anything was possible. She even made cheerleading trips abroad, encouraging Americans to join Britain's side in the war and Russians to fight even harder.

Emmeline had swapped the suffragettes' purple, white and green for the red, white and blue of the British Union Jack, and the Government was massively relieved to find her fighting alongside them, rather than against them. But some suffragettes and many suffragists thought all warfare was **just plain wrong**. They were proud to be British, but wanted no killing done in their name. So Emmeline's new fighting talk on behalf of the Government sickened them. Even Sylvia criticized her, and so did Adela from faraway Australia, though mum was in no mood to listen: she said their views made her ashamed.

But while Emmeline might have shelved her own suffrage campaign, not everyone else had . . .

THE GOVERNMENT SAYS THANK YOU

As the war dragged on, more people began to see that votes for women might actually be a good thing.

After all, without women doing so many vital jobs, the country could not have kept ticking over. Even Mr Asquith couldn't deny that.

Then, half way through the war, Britain got a new Prime Minister: Mr David Lloyd George, the politician whose house Emmeline had once plotted to blow up! Luckily he didn't bear a grudge. In fact he'd already been doing more than many MPs to get women what they wanted, and in 1916 it was finally agreed that Parliament would bring in a new law. At long, long last, and partly as a kind of reward for all their efforts during the war, **8.5 million British women** would be allowed to vote!!!

You might have expected Emmeline to be ecstatic. Of course this was a brilliant breakthrough for Britain's women. But it wasn't quite as brilliant as Emmeline had been hoping.

For one thing, women had to be patient once again. The new law didn't come in until 1918, when Britain's side finally won the world war. And even then, there still wasn't true equality between male and female voters. This was because **women had to be over 30** years of age to vote, whereas **men only had to be 21**, or even as young as 19 if they'd fought in the war. So as a result of all that:

12.5 million men now had the vote – which was a whole lot more than 8.5 million women.

Emmeline could have ranted and raved about that, but she didn't. At 60 years of age, she was full of aches and pains, and some of her old fury had died down. But most importantly, for the first time ever in British history women could vote.

With her main job now done, Emmeline closed down the Union and she led a new 'Women's Party' with Christabel. They demanded equal rights for women and men in every area of life – as workers, wage-earners, partners in marriage, and as parents. It seemed a startling idea in 1918 and even today **women are still fighting for these rights**.

Christabel tried to become Britain's first female MP under the Women's Party banner. But like her dad before her, she didn't win her seat – even after the votes had to be totted up **a second time** (because Christabel claimed the male election officers couldn't count properly!). Both women were so disheartened, they decided to wind up the Women's Party. Perhaps it was just too far ahead of its time.

Emmeline – The Comeback

Emmeline's life was still pretty full. Astonishingly, she had found herself **a whole new Team Pankhurst** to lead. Back in 1915, while the world war still raged, she'd tried to get the Union to set up a special home for 50 'war babies' – children who had lost their parents as a result of the fighting. That plan turned out to be too expensive to work. But, determined as ever to be as helpful as she could, Emmeline took four three-year-old orphan girls into her own home.

Don't worry about the little ones, I will take care of them.

Nanny Pine

Joan Pembridge

Mary Gordon

Elizabeth Tudor

Kathleen King

She was usually too busy to look after this new family herself. First she had her war work, then as an ex-suffragette megastar she went on treks around the USA and Canada talking to paying audiences about the challenges women still faced. Christabel lent a hand with the girls whenever she was around, and Catherine Pine – the nurse who'd helped Emmeline recover from her hunger strikes – became their nanny. In the end, though, Emmeline couldn't really earn enough to support them all. So with a sad heart **she arranged for each girl in turn to be adopted** by rich families.

After a short, unsuccessful effort at running a teashop in France – shopkeeping really wasn't her thing – Emmeline headed back to Britain in 1926. Almost any other woman would now have put her feet up. She knew lots of rich women from the old days and they offered to pay to give her a comfortable old age, but she was far too proud to accept hand-outs. Instead, she took one last shot at the political big time, throwing herself into a bid to become a Conservative MP in the East End of London.

She gave it everything she'd got, making speech after speech as if her life depended on it. For nearly 70 years, whatever Emmeline did, she'd believed she could never be beaten, but eventually even she had to admit that this time she had bitten off more than she could chew.

Ever since her hunger strikes, she had been plagued by jaundice. Before the election could take place, the illness made her very sick indeed and as Easter

1928 approached she was forced to put her campaign on hold.

Then things got worse. As well as jaundice and stomach problems, she seemed to have blood poisoning. Her doctors tried their best but couldn't help . . .

EMMELINE HEARS SOMETHING WONDERFUL

Emmeline took to her bed in a small stuffy room over a London hairdresser's shop. She had made herself world famous, but had **never made a fortune**, so she couldn't afford to rent anywhere more comfortable.

Her doctors kept telling her she had to rest, and she did feel terribly tired, but it was hard to sleep with such pains in her stomach, and with motor cars roaring past outside in the street, and the female staff down below in the hairdresser's making such a racket.

Yet Emmeline still managed a quiet smile. How different life had been in her youth, she thought – no cars or buses on the roads, and men having all the fun. In those days, men hadn't trusted women to do anything. She smiled again as she remembered a true story about a hairdresser that she'd heard as a girl:

That was all in the past. In the last few years so many new opportunities had opened up for women. They were now allowed to study at universities just like men. They could work as lawyers and policewomen and do top office jobs. As teachers, they still didn't earn quite as much as men but they were getting there. And of course, since 1918, women had been able to vote in elections to Parliament – and by 1923, **eight MPs actually were women**. Things were changing so much for the better.

But something still nagged at Emmeline. She had campaigned for equal suffrage – for women to have exactly the same rights as men. But while men aged 21 and over could vote, women still had to be 30.

The suffrage protests had not stopped completely, and plenty of MPs agreed that things should be evened up. But any new law had to get the go-ahead from both the House of Commons and the House of Lords. So the discussions in Parliament went on and on. Emmeline had gone along to listen to some of them – and not for the first time she felt frustrated. A truly fair deal for women still seemed just out of reach.

As the month of May 1928 drew to a close, sleepless on her sickbed, Emmeline gave a sigh . . .

Then downstairs it all went quiet. Someone had come in off the street with news that **stopped everyone in their tracks**. Emmeline could almost hear the hairdressers holding their breath. Pushing herself up in the bed, she strained to hear the message too. But only the first few words reached her before everyone below started clapping and shrieking. With that, Emmeline sank back into her pillows, smiling from ear to ear. The first few words had been enough. It was the best message ever:

PARLIAMENT HAS MADE THE LAW!

The icing was on the cake. All adult women had got their vote, and women would now count just as much as men. From this point on, **everyone** aged 21 and over would be able to take part in elections. They'd finally **put the `get´ into `suffragette´**!

And so, just days from the end of her amazing roller-coaster ride of a life, Emmeline gave a deep, relieved sigh. She had never lost faith. She'd always believed this would happen one day. Now it had.

FAREWELL TO THE WORLD

Later that month Emmeline grew so ill with influenza that she was moved into a nursing home. Only Christabel was allowed to visit her. And on 14th June the awesome story of Britain's greatest female protestor drew to its close.

News of her death spread fast. Emmeline had always fizzed so much with life, it seemed impossible she was gone. Across the globe people paid their respects – even the ones who'd bitterly disagreed with her while she lived. All she had in the bank at the end was £86 and there are no prizes for guessing who she left it to. Yes, Christabel. Of course, her favourite daughter attended Emmeline's London funeral on 18th June. Sylvia came too, with a brand new baby son. Adela didn't make it from Australia, where she now had her own big brood of kids who never got to meet their grandma.

Well over a thousand other people were there that day. Most of them were women – young and old, rich and poor, many in suffragette dress. All the way from Westminster to Brompton Cemetery crowds watched the hearse pass by, with a column of old Union comrades marching behind it. When Emmeline's coffin was finally lowered into the ground, friends stepped up to throw flowers into her grave. **Purple irises, white lilies, green leaves**.

I only wish I could have been there to see it.

REMEMBERING EMMELINE

Memories of Emmeline – some fond, some not so fond – lived on long after she was buried. It was bound to happen – she'd stirred up the world so much.

Huge crowds gathered again on the day in 1930 that Prime Minister Stanley Baldwin unveiled a life-sized bronze statue of her in Victoria Tower Gardens, close to the Houses of Parliament in central London.

It was a very good likeness. As if by magic, there Emmeline stood again, with one arm slightly raised to rouse her audience. A police band played some of her old friend Ethel Smyth's music. Not long before, many of these policemen had grappled hand to hand with suffragettes – now **some of them wept** as they remembered the Union's feisty little leader who would never take no for an answer. They respected her now. She really had made a difference.

Almost a century later, Emmeline's statue still stands in the Gardens, a painting of her hangs in London's National Portrait Gallery too; and still today, the world over, women and men and girls and boys can be inspired by her great example.

Emmeline And The Great Shake-Up

Hardly anything in history happens because of just one person or group of people. Emmeline Pankhurst didn't win the vote for women single-handed. Her war didn't even bring complete equality between women and men. Many women today still have to strive to get the same chances in life as men, and the same pay for their work.

But because in the early 1900s there was just too much poverty, too much suffering, too much misery and such terrible inequality, a furious Emmeline took her army onto the streets and she caused **the most almighty shake-up**.

Emmeline's suffragettes helped to make men look at women differently. They helped women to look at themselves differently too. After Emmeline, women no longer had to think they were second best, young girls no longer had to see themselves as 'inferior' to boys, and no father had any excuse to look at his daughter and say—

'What a pity she wasn't born a lad.'

Ah, I thought you might want the last word.

And my very last word is this: every girl and boy in the land can make a difference, if only they are willing to fight. Say no to any kind of inequality. Wherever you see unfairness, try to stamp it out. And never forget all those battles we suffragettes fought. Our goal was to make sure that one day EVERYONE would have the chance to change things for the better too - by voting!

Index

Use these pages for a quick reference!

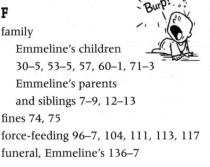

Don't close the book! I haven't had MY say yet!